SCIENCE
ESSENTIALS
CHEMISTRY

Materials

DENISE WALKER

Evans

EVANS

LONDON

© Evans Brothers Ltd 2007

Published by:
Evans Brothers
2a Portman Mansions
Chiltern Street
London W1U 6NR

Series editor:
Harriet Brown

Editor:
Katie Harker

Design:
Simon Morse

Illustrations:
Ian Thompson, Simon Morse

Printed in China by
WKT Company Limited

British Library Cataloguing in
Publication Data

 Walker, Denise
 Materials. - (Science essentials.
 Chemistry)
 1. Chemicals - Juvenile literature
 I. Title
 542

ISBN-10: 0-23752-998-X

ISBN-13: 978-0-23752-998-7

Contents

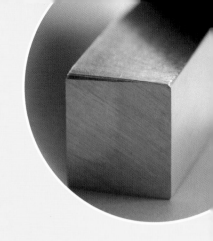

Introduction

Our world is made up of many different substances. Thanks to the work of chemists, we are able to make sense of the objects around us. We are surrounded by solids, liquids and gases which are very different in the way that they look and behave. But these physical states all have one thing in common. They are made from tiny particles – the building blocks of every material that we know.

This book takes you on a journey to discover more about the wonderful world of materials. Find out what substances are made from, discover the way in which particles behave and look at how we can make new substances of our own. You can also find out about famous scientists, like Ernest Rutherford and Dimitri Mendeleev. Learn how they used their skills to discover the existence of particles and to find patterns in the behaviour of the materials around us.

This book also contains feature boxes that will help you to unravel more about the mysteries of materials. Test yourself on what you have learnt so far; investigate some of the concepts discussed; find out more key facts; and discover some of the scientific findings of the past and how these might be utilised in the future.

Materials are all around us. Now you can understand why objects look and behave in the way that they do.

1

What is matter?

The world around us is composed of millions of different types of things. We are surrounded by a vast number of solid items, as well as many liquids and gases. These different substances have various properties and ways of behaving. We use some solids as building materials, liquids can be poured into a glass and some gases help us to breathe. Many objects can be broken down into smaller items – people, for example, are composed of bones, blood and muscles. Chemists study the enormous range of materials in the world and try to explain the changes that take place around us.

▲ Thales believed that water was the basic element from which all things originated. Other philosophers disagreed, claiming that the basic element was air or fire.

WHERE DO MATERIALS COME FROM?

This was a question considered by the ancient Greeks in 600 **BCE**. Although today, scientists carry out practical experiments to test their ideas, Greek philosophers preferred to discuss ideas to help them to explain the behaviour of the world around them.

At the time, the Greeks knew how to extract metals from rocks, and they used fire to change the properties of materials. One Greek philosopher, called Thales, suggested that all substances were made from smaller parts that he called elements. Thales believed that when one substance was turned into another, the elements (and therefore the properties of that material) changed.

Other Greek philosophers disagreed with Thales. Anaximander, for example, thought that the elements themselves did not change, but instead were in competition with each other. Anaximander suggested that all forms of matter were continually changing because the elements had to wrestle for dominance.

After much debate, in 400 BCE, Greek philosophers, such as Plato and Aristotle, suggested that there were four types of elements – air, water, earth and fire. They believed that each of these elements had properties that explained the different materials they produced. For example, 'earth' elements, such as metals, had the properties of dryness and coldness and 'air' elements, such as gases, had the properties of heat and moistness. This theory became the basis of western thinking about the natural world for over 2,000 years, until the rise

▲▼ Earth, air, fire and water
were considered to be the basic
elements from which all things
were made – until the 1700s,
when chemists discovered the
existence of many
more elements.

of chemistry in the 1700s
(when chemists began to study
the composition of rocks and
minerals and realised that
there were not just four
elements but many!). In other
parts of the world, different
elements were suggested. In India, for example,
five elements were proposed – space, air, fire,
water and earth. In China, philosophers also
spoke of five elements – but this time they were
earth, wood, metal, fire and water. Even today,
these five 'qualities' form the basis of many
Chinese and complementary medical practices.

DISCOVERING PARTICLES

Whilst Plato and Aristotle were discussing the
elements, another Greek philosopher,
Democritus, suggested the theory that all matter
was made up of tiny particles that were so small
they could not be seen. Democritus believed that
the types of particle, and the way in which they
were arranged, determined the final properties of a
material. Many people did not believe Democritus
because he could not provide evidence for his
theory. Today, however, scientific experiments
have indicated the existence of particles.

If particles are too small to be seen with the naked
eye (or even with the most powerful of
microscopes) how do we know that they actually
exist? The answer is that we don't, but scientific
experiments have strongly indicated that matter
is made up of particles. Scientists build theories
from scientific evidence and as time passes these
theories are either proved or disproved. In the
case of particle theory, evidence is still being
collected, but the theory has yet to be refuted.

Some of the evidence for the existence of particles can be found around us. Smoke from a fire or a barbecue, for example, does not travel through the air in a straight line, but rather weaves its way slowly into the atmosphere. Particle theory explains that both smoke and air are made from tiny particles. As the smoke particles move, they collide with particles in the air and slightly change their direction. This appears to us as a random smoke trail.

BROWNIAN MOTION

Scientists can create the behaviour of smoke in a laboratory. First, smoke is introduced into a small box called a smoke cell. The smoke cell is then viewed under a microscope and very small particles can actually be seen moving around. This phenomenon was first observed by the Scottish scientist Robert Brown in the early 1800s and is called **Brownian Motion**. If a bottle of perfume is spilt, people on the other side of the room will soon be able to smell the fragrance. This is because the scent in the perfume **evaporates** and travels through the air by a process called diffusion (see page 20). The scent particles travel in exactly the same way as the smoke particles.

▲ The rising smoke from a bonfire indicates that particles of smoke collide with particles of air.

TIME TRAVEL: INTO THE FUTURE

▶ Atomic force microscopy (AFM) is a technique for observing matter that will become widely used in the future. An atomic force microscope doesn't use a lens, like a traditional microscope, but instead uses a probe (or 'tip') that scans very close to an object's surface, to measure properties such as height and magnetism. When the tip encounters a tiny change of surface it moves a lever.

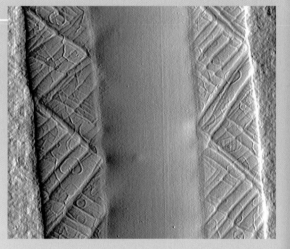

▲ AFM images help scientists observe materials, such as this polymer film, more closely than ever before.

▲ This scientist is using an atomic force microscope to observe the surface of an object in minute detail.

This makes it possible to take measurements over a very small area. A laser beam senses these changes and records them as a map, almost like a 'photographic' picture. The microscope 'feels' the surface of a sample with such a sensitive touch that it can sometimes even sense the individual atoms on the surface of a crystal, such as gold.

Looking inside the atom

2

Thanks to the work of many scientists during the 1800s and 1900s (see pages 10-11), we now know that the substances in the world around us are made from minute particles called **atoms**. We also know that there are three types of particle inside an atom. Today, the modern model of the atom is based on what scientists have discovered about the arrangement of these particles.

THE PARTICLES OF AN ATOM

About 100 years ago, scientists began to investigate what makes one substance different from another. They began by identifying the properties of atoms. Using a beam of **radioactive** particles, called '**alpha particles**', they found that almost all the mass of an atom was found at its centre, which they called the **nucleus**. The nucleus was found to contain smaller particles called **protons** and **neutrons**. Protons had a positive electric charge, while neutrons had no charge at all.

Atoms have a neutral charge overall so they must contain a negative charge that counteracts the positive charge of the protons. It is the **electrons** that carry this negative charge. Electrons circle the nucleus at varying distances. They are attracted to the positively-charged nucleus, but because they are constantly moving and relatively light, they stay at these distances ,which we call electron 'shells'. This arrangement of particles has been likened to planets orbiting the Sun in our Solar System. Although the planets are attracted by the Sun's gravitational pull, they stay in orbit because they are moving so quickly. Scientists now know that substances differ because they have a particular arrangement of protons, neutrons and electrons.

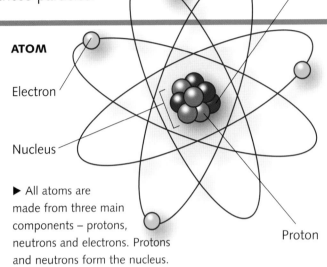

ATOM

Electron

Nucleus

Neutron

Proton

▶ All atoms are made from three main components – protons, neutrons and electrons. Protons and neutrons form the nucleus.

Summary

Particle	Relative mass	Relative charge
Proton	1	+1
Neutron	1	0
Electron	1/1800	−1

▲ The particles of an atom are extremely light so scientists tend to explain their mass using relative terms.

DID YOU KNOW?

▶ If a sports stadium was an atom, the nucleus would be about the size of a grape in the centre circle. Consider the Yankee Stadium, USA (below) or Wembley stadium in the UK.

Time travel: What are particles made of?

All the materials in the world around us are made from tiny particles that we cannot see with the naked eye. The arrangement of these particles explains why some materials are solids whereas others are liquids or gases. But what are these tiny particles made of? The work of four scientists in particular have helped to answer this question.

John Dalton (1766-1844)

John Dalton was an English chemist who used the work of Greek philosophers (such as Democritus, see page 7) and other scientists (such as Antoine Lavoisier and Joseph Louis Proust) to study the effects of combining two substances to make a new material.

Dalton's work provided scientists with some basic rules about the behaviour of particles. His 'atomic theory' stated that:

▶ All matter is composed of minute particles, called atoms.
▶ Atoms cannot be divided into smaller parts and cannot be destroyed.
▶ Atoms of any element all have the same mass and properties. These atoms differ from substance to substance.
▶ Atoms combine together in simple ratios to form new substances. Dalton called these '**compounds**'.

◀ The work of John Dalton was the first published theory suggesting that substances were made from particles. Dalton's ideas were crucial to the development of future work on particle theory.

J J Thomson (1856-1940)

Joseph John Thomson was an English physicist working at Cambridge University. Thomson explored what particles could be made from, in an attempt to look inside the atom. He experimented using currents of electricity (which we now call cathode rays) travelling through empty glass tubes. Thomson noticed that these currents of electricity changed direction if they were positioned next to a magnet.

▲ Cathode rays are attracted by a magnetic force. This is because they contain electron particles that are negatively-charged.

From these observations, Thomson proposed that he was observing streams of particles that were smaller components of atoms (rather than the movement of atoms themselves). This was a very bold suggestion because, at the time, scientists believed that atoms were the basic unit of matter and could not be divided into smaller parts.

Thomson's suggestion was investigated by teams of scientists over many years and we now know that cathode rays are streams of electricity made up of electrons – very small, negatively-charged particles that are fundamental parts of every atom. The electrons changed direction in the presence of magnets because they had a negative charge. Thomson had discovered the negative part of an atom, but he did not know what the inside of an atom looked like. At the time, he proposed his 'plum pudding' theory. This described the atom as a bed of positive charge (the sponge) in which negative charges (the plums) could be found.

Ernest Rutherford (1871-1937)

Ernest Rutherford was born in New Zealand but worked for some time at Cambridge University in the UK. Rutherford helped to discover the nucleus and to identify the positive part of an atom.

In one of his experiments, Rutherford shone alpha particles (positively-charged particles composed of two protons and two neutrons) onto thin pieces of gold. When the alpha particles hit and rebounded from the gold atoms, Rutherford captured their path using a zinc sulphide screen. Each time the screen was hit by an alpha particle, the positive charge caused the zinc to spark. Rutherford made some staggering observations:

▶ Most of the alpha particles went straight through the gold leaf, to reach the screen on the other side. From this Rutherford concluded that most of the gold atoms consisted of space.

▶ Some alpha particles appeared to go through the gold leaf, but were slightly deflected before they hit the screen. From this Rutherford concluded that part of the atom was positive and repelled the alpha particles as they passed close by.

▶ Amazingly, a very small number of alpha particles rebounded in the direction from which they came.

THE GOLD LEAF EXPERIMENT

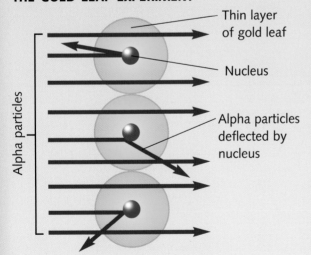

▲ Rutherford's experiment revealed that the gold atoms had a small, dense area in the middle. He called this the nucleus.

From his experiments, Rutherford concluded that the atom was not like J.J Thomson's plum pudding theory, but instead was mostly space with a small positive charge in the middle. He called this positive component the proton and the middle of the atom the nucleus.

Niels Bohr (1885-1962)

Niels Bohr was a Danish physicist who worked alongside Rutherford at the University of Manchester in the early 1900s. Bohr bombarded the atoms of various elements using cathode rays. He observed what happened to the atoms' negatively-charged electrons and discovered that different elements produced a slightly different pattern. He also noticed that if the energy of the collisions was reduced, the atoms' electrons moved at a slower pace.

From his observations, Bohr was able to deduce that electrons were found in discrete shells surrounding the nucleus of an atom. When the electrons were bombarded with cathode rays, they were able to jump from one shell to the next because they gained energy. When they lost this energy, visible light was emitted. Bohr found that the electrons would not jump to other electron shells if they did not receive the correct amount of energy. This began the important basis of quantum theory (about the emission and absorption of energy by matter) that scientists use today.

The work of Dalton, Thomson, Rutherford and Bohr was an outstanding contribution to our understanding of the material word. However, despite the rapid advancement of their ideas, modern atomic theory was not fully accepted by the scientific community until the early 1900s.

INVESTIGATE

▶ There are many other important scientists, both past and present, who have contributed to the model of the atom that is used today. Research either Albert Einstein or James Chadwick to find out what contributions they have made.

UNDERSTANDING HOW ATOMS DIFFER

We now know that elements differ because they have a unique number of protons, neutrons and electrons. To help us to recognise this difference more easily, scientists have assigned two numbers to elements. The larger number is called the **mass number** (or 'atomic mass'). This represents the total number of protons and neutrons in the nucleus of an element's atom. The smaller number is called the **atomic number**. This represents just the number of protons contained in the atom. Since atoms have a neutral charge, we assume that the number of protons is equal to the number of electrons (because they have equal, but opposite charges).

For example, the metal lithium has been assigned an atomic number of 3 and a mass number of 7. This means that lithium atoms have three protons (atomic number), three electrons (equivalent to atomic number) and four neutrons (mass number minus atomic number). Similarly, the metal beryllium has been assigned an atomic

▲◀ Lithium (above) and beryllium (left) are both metals but their varying atomic structure means that they have very different properties.

number of 4 and a mass number of 9. This means that beryllium atoms have four protons, four electrons and five neutrons. Because lithium and beryllium atoms have a different number of protons, neutrons and electrons, the metals have very different properties.

DID YOU KNOW?

▶ Scientists in Switzerland have shown that it is possible for two identical particles to respond simultaneously to a stimulus that one particle receives, even if they are over ten kilometres apart. The scientists at the University of Geneva split particles of light, called photons, into pairs and sent them down separate optical fibres (telephone lines). Despite being separated by a number of kilometres, each particle chose the same path down their respective optical fibre. The experiment confirms a theory that Austrian physicist Erwin Schrödinger predicted – that entangled particles (particles that are formed at the same time and have identical properties) echo each other's actions, no matter how far apart they are. Scientists think that a change to one particle, will affect the other, even if it is on the opposite side of the Universe.

INVESTIGATE

▶ Research the atomic number and the mass number of each of the following elements. How many protons, neutrons and electrons do atoms of each element have?

(1) Magnesium
(2) Bromine
(3) Neon

Time travel: Discoveries of the past

Since the modern model of the atom was proposed by Bohr in 1913, scientists have been wondering whether there are more than just three types of atomic particle. As experimental technology has developed, this search has brought many new discoveries.

In 1995, for example, the Nobel prize for physics was awarded to two separate research centres, in California, USA, for the discovery of two of the smallest particles in the Universe. During the 1950s, Frederick Reines and his colleagues at the University of California were able to demonstrate the existence of a particle called the '**neutrino**' (the 'little neutral one'). This particle has no mass or electrical charge and is therefore very difficult to detect. Scientists had proposed its existence, however, because they noticed the presence of mystery particles, produced when radioactive materials decayed. In the 1950s, Reines and his colleague, Clyde Cowan, set out to prove the existence of the neutrino.

In 1956, working at the Savannah River nuclear reactor, 12 metres underground, Reines and Cowan succeeded in discovering the neutrino. The scientists waited for what they believed to be a neutrino particle from a nuclear reaction, to hit a tank of water. The water contained cadmium chloride – cadmium chloride is highly soluble in water. It also absorbs particles easily and when it does so it emits high-frequency electromagnetic radiation, which can be detected. Reines and Cowan confirmed the existence of the neutrino by observing these changes following a nuclear reaction. Today, scientists believe that neutrinos affect the motion of galaxies and play a key role in the nuclear fusion burning of stars (see page 29).

Then, in 1977, another subatomic particle (the 'tau'), was discovered by Martin Perl and his colleagues at Stanford University. Perl and his team conducted a series of experiments spanning three years, which recorded the effects of colliding different particles. During these experiments, the team discovered a mystery particle that was electrically charged, about 3,500 times heavier than an electron and had a very short lifetime. The particle was later named the 'tau'.

Today, similar collision experiments are carried out in Switzerland at the European Centre for Nuclear Research (CERN). Here, particles of all descriptions are bombarded and collided for research groups who are constantly searching for new particles. The centre is made up of a large circular tunnel (27 kilometres in circumference) beneath the mountains. Around the edges of the tunnel are 5,000 magnets that are used to make circling particles move faster. To date, 12 subatomic particles have been discovered and the latest of these is called the top quark. The top quark is a very heavy particle that existed for a brief time following the creation of the Universe. In 1992, a large team of international scientists mimicked this explosion by colliding trillions of subatomic particles together at CERN, and proved the existence of the top quark.

▼ Specialist equipment has been installed in underground tunnels at CERN near Geneva, Switzerland, to investigate atomic particles.

In the early 1900s, Niels Bohr put forward a theory to explain how electrons are arranged in the atom (see page 11). He suggested that electrons were positioned around the nucleus at varying distances. And that these 'shells' of electrons had a particular level of energy (electron shells are sometimes called 'energy levels'). Bohr thought it was possible to move an electron from one shell to another by applying an exact amount of energy. His ideas formed the basis of many modern theories about the behaviour of electrons in atoms.

Thanks to Bohr's theory, scientists have discovered some interesting patterns in electron behaviour. For example, the electron shells in any atom have been found to have the following properties:

▶ Each electron shell contains electrons that have the same energy.

▶ Electron shells nearest to the nucleus have the lowest energy.

▶ Electron shells with the lowest energy fill first.

▶ Electron shells furthest from the nucleus have smaller energy gaps between them than those nearest to the nucleus.

▶ Each electron shell holds a maximum number of electrons. Some of these are shown below.

Electron shell	Maximum number of electrons
1st (nearest to nucleus)	2
2nd	8
3rd	18

▶ The electrons nearest to the nucleus are very difficult to remove because they are strongly attracted to the positive charge of the nucleus.

ELECTRON SHELLS

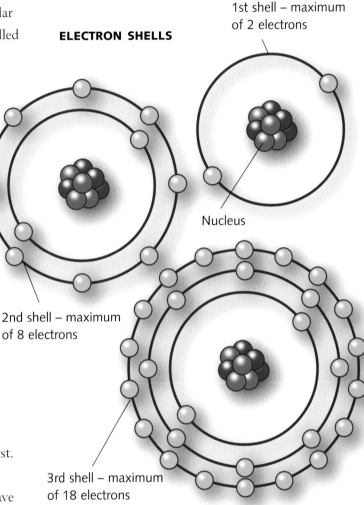

1st shell – maximum of 2 electrons

Nucleus

2nd shell – maximum of 8 electrons

3rd shell – maximum of 18 electrons

▲ Electrons are arranged around the nucleus at varying distances. We call these 'electron shells'. The electrons have increasing levels of energy as they move away from the nucleus.

ELECTRON CONFIGURATION

Different atoms have a different number of occupied electron shells. For example, hydrogen atoms have one occupied electron shell, while uranium atoms have seven. The way in which electrons are arranged in the atom is called the **electron configuration**. The atomic number tells us the number of protons (and therefore electrons) in the atom (see page 12). We can extend this idea to calculate the electron configuration of the atom. For example, carbon has an atomic number of 6 (and therefore six protons and six electrons). Electrons always fill the shells nearest to the nucleus first. However, because there can only be a maximum of two electrons in the first electron shell, the remaining four electrons move to the second shell (this shell is not completely full because a maximum of eight electrons can be positioned at this level). We write the electron configuration for carbon as 2.4.

(see page 12)

A CARBON ATOM

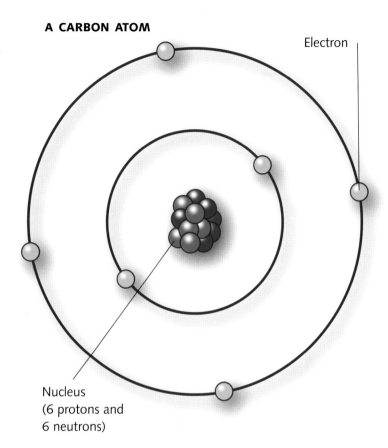

Electron

Nucleus
(6 protons and
6 neutrons)

TEST YOURSELF

▶ Aluminium has an atomic number of 13. What is the electron configuration for aluminium?

THE IMPORTANCE OF ELECTRON CONFIGURATION

The substances around us are formed when elements combine to form **molecules** and compounds (see page 35). The atoms in molecules and compounds join when electrons move within and between atoms during a chemical reaction. Electrons and protons have opposite charges and they are well balanced if they are equal in number. However, if these charges become imbalanced, the electrons rearrange themselves between atoms so that they become more stable. Some atoms share electrons to become a new substance, whilst others give away electrons (or remove electrons from other atoms). In some cases, this rearrangement links the atoms together to form molecules. We call this **bonding**. During chemical bonding, atoms always try to achieve the maximum number of electrons on their outer shells.

(see page 35)

Chemical reactions are different from nuclear reactions. Chemical reactions are caused by a change in electron configuration whereas nuclear reactions are caused by a change in the nucleus of an atom (with protons and neutrons either lost or gained). Chemists are most interested in chemical reactions and try to explain these reactions using the theory of electron configuration.

INVESTIGATE

▶ Research the atomic number of the following atoms and work out their electron configurations:

(1) Neon

(4) Chlorine

(2) Magnesium

(5) Sodium

(3) Calcium

Solids, liquids and gases

Many substances in the world around us are 'solids'. These materials have a number of similar properties. Solids tend to hold their shape unless a force is applied. The clothes that we wear and the chairs we sit on are solids. These materials have a particular shape. We use other solids as building materials. These solids are strong enough to withstand storms and high winds. All solids need a certain degree of strength and it is this property that mainly distinguishes solids from liquids and gases.

A CLOSER LOOK AT SOLIDS

If we could observe solids from an atomic point of view, we would see that the particles are packed closely together.

According to 'particle theory' (see page 7) the particles in solids are arranged in tightly fixed and regular positions. The particles are held in these positions by strong forces. We call these 'intermolecular forces of attraction'. They occur when the protons of one atom attract the electrons of another atom. Although the particles are not free to leave their positions, they can vibrate about a fixed point.

This arrangement of particles means that solids have the following properties:

▶ Solids are usually strong because when we press them, the strong forces of attraction between the atoms cannot easily be broken.

▶ Solids keep their shape because the particles are held so firmly together – they can only vibrate.

▶ Solids cannot be poured because the particles are held together and do not separate from each other.

▶ Solids do not exert any pressure if they are contained. Because a solid's particles are not free to move like a gas, they cannot exert any pressure against the sides of a container.

◀ The atoms of a solid are held closely together by intermolecular forces of attraction – the protons of one atom attract the electrons of another atom.

All the solids in the world around us demonstrate these properties. However, some solids are a bit more difficult to interpret. Can you think of any examples?

Sand is a solid, despite the fact that it can be poured. If you examine sand carefully you will see that it is made up of very small solid grains. Sand grains cannot be poured individually, but collectively sand can be poured.

Custard is a liquid but it can also demonstrate some solid properties. If custard is made from flour (which has a starch base) it can be made so that it is strong enough to walk on. A custard mixture of this kind is unable to withstand a very large amount of pressure, however. If you stopped walking on the custard, the force of your weight in one area, would mean that you'd quickly sink in!

TEST YOURSELF

▶ In what ways can each of the following substances be described as a solid? In what ways are they not typical solids?

(1) Jelly

(2) Adhesive paste

(3) Glue stick

◀ ▲ Custard is a liquid, but it can be made so that it is strong enough to walk on. If you stop walking, however, you quickly sink in!

DID YOU KNOW?

▶ Have you seen films showing cowboys sinking and perishing in quicksand? It looks frightening but, scientifically, quicksand isn't quite as dangerous as it seems. Quicksand occurs wherever there's sand (or soil) and water. The sand stays solid when the individual grains are in contact with each other, but when sand becomes saturated with water the grains no longer touch and begin to move around and act rather like a liquid. Quicksand looks solid, but when someone steps on it they sink because the water is pushed up through the sand and the grains become separated. If the person then starts to struggle, this process is enhanced and they sink even further. However, sand is denser than water, so you actually float better in saturated sand, than in water. If the cowboys had stopped struggling, they would have been able to float until help came.

▲ Quicksand looks solid enough to walk on but can be dangerous if you start to sink!

A CLOSER LOOK AT LIQUIDS

Like solids, liquids are all around us, too. About 70 per cent of the Earth's surface is covered in ocean water and almost two-thirds of the human body contains water. But liquids have distinctly different properties to solids – they allow solids to pass through them. Marine animals swim through ocean water to survive and blood circulates around the body to keep us alive. Liquids also flow from one place to another under the influence of gravity. If we could observe liquids from an atomic point of view, we would see that liquid particles are more spread out than solid particles.

'Particle theory' shows that liquid particles are held together in small groups because most of the strong intermolecular forces of attraction present in solids have been broken down. Liquid particles contain a little more energy than solid particles, giving them a greater ability to move. The small groups of liquid particles can slide past each other, but because there are still some forces of attraction present, the particles are not completely free to move around. This arrangement of particles means that liquids have the following properties:

▶ Liquids cannot hold objects because they are not strong. If we touch a liquid, our hand will pass through. This is because there are few forces of attraction between the particles.

▶ Liquids cannot keep their shape. This is because the particles are free to move. Liquids will fill and take on the shape of the container that they are stored in.

▶ Liquids can be poured because the particles are free to move around one another.

▶ Liquids can be compressed slightly because pressure pushes the particles closer together. For example, if you take a syringe that is half filled with water and block the end, when you try to push the plunger down, the water will be compressed slightly because it is pushed into a smaller space.

▶ Small quantities of liquids do not exert much pressure. This is because the particles are not completely free to move and collide with the wall of a container. If the container is filled completely, however, the liquid exerts more pressure. The water pressure also increases with the amount of water in a container. For example, water pressure at the bottom of the seabed is huge. There are not many marine animals at this depth because their bodies would be crushed by the force of the water.

▼ The atoms in a liquid are free to move around but are held together in groups by intermolecular forces.

Unusual liquids

Some of the liquids around us are described as 'volatile'. This means that they turn into gases quite easily. For example, we smell petrol fumes at a petrol station because petrol is a volatile liquid and some of its particles evaporate rapidly into the air. Other liquids are described as being non-volatile. Treacle, for example, is a thick, syrup-like substance that can be poured slowly, but will not evaporate.

The difference between petrol and treacle is due to the differences in 'stickiness' of the various particles in these liquids. In petrol, the particles are arranged in smaller groups than in treacle. With fewer intermolecular forces of attraction, the petrol particles are freer to evaporate. In contrast, the groups of particles in treacle become entangled together, making this liquid difficult to pour.

▲ This glass blower is changing the shape of a glass object. When solid glass is heated to a high temperature it behaves like a liquid and can be manipulated.

Glass objects, such as ornaments and windows, are made from liquid glass that cools to become a solid. To make an ornament, a glass blower moulds the liquid mixture before it is allowed to cool. Some glass windows can 'melt' on very hot days. Scientists have found that, in hot weather, the thickness of a pane of glass can become thinner at the top and thicker at the bottom. However, this movement is unnoticeable without the use of precision instruments.

Mercury is an unusual metal because it is liquid at room temperature (metals are usually thought of as strong, hard materials). Mercury is so heavy and dense that objects such as bricks and lumps of lead can float in it! Mercury freezes at about -38°C and boils at about 357°C.

A CLOSER LOOK AT GASES

The air around us, and that fills our lungs, is probably the gas that we are most familiar with. Air displays many of the properties explained by particle theory. The air cannot be seen, smelt or tasted and we often take its presence for granted. However, gases such as air play a very important role in our survival. Let's look at the properties of gases in more detail.

Gases have a much more random arrangement of particles than liquids and solids. Particle theory tells us that there are no forces of attraction between gas particles and that the particles contain much more energy than those in liquids and solids. Gas particles are constantly moving around and if we could see them, they would have a random appearance – no two gases, at any one moment, have exactly the same arrangement of particles.

▼ The atoms in a gas are free to move around because there are no forces of attraction holding them together.

This arrangement of particles means that gases have the following properties:

▶ There are no forces of attraction between gas particles. We cannot press or sit on a gas because there are no forces keeping the particles together. When we touch a gas, the particles move away from our fingers.

▶ Gases do not keep their shape. This is because the particles move to fill the container they are stored in. Every gas particle has its own path and plenty of energy to keep it on the move. When gas particles meet the wall of a container (or each other) they simply bounce off and pursue a new path.

▶ Most gases cannot be poured. The particles in gases are free to move around and are therefore difficult to contain (it is only possible to pour a gas if it is a dense gas being poured into a less dense gas).

▶ Gases exert pressure. Gas particles constantly move around and collide with the walls of their container. As they do so, they exert a pressure. The more gas particles present the more the pressure increases. The tyres of a car, for example, are filled with air – when the tyres are inflated, the tyre pressure is said to increase.

▶ Gases can diffuse. This means that they travel from an area where there is a lot of gas, to an area where there is very little. Perfume scents travel through the air by a process of diffusion. Diffusion occurs in the animal world, too. Many animals can detect each other by the chemicals they secrete.

These chemicals evaporate into gases and although they are very dilute, they can be detected from very long distances. Some moths, for example, can detect scents from up to five kilometres away, from which they find a mate. Dogs and cats also use a scent to mark their territory.

▶ Gases can be compressed. Gas particles have a lot of space between them, although they are constantly moving at high speed. This is because the forces of attraction holding the particles together are overcome by the energy of the moving particles. If a gas is trapped within a container and pressed, the particles move together and can be compressed. If the particles move close enough together, the compressed gas becomes a liquid. Some gases, such as butane, are compressed and stored as liquids because this takes up less space and makes them easier to transport.

◀ Camping gas is compressed into a liquid so that it can be stored and transported easily.

▼ This satellite map shows the extent of the smoke cloud after the Buncefield Oil depot explosion, which drifted at an altitude of 3,000 metres, covering much of southern England.

▲ The Buncefield Oil Depot fire in 2005 produced smoke covering an area of more than 120 kilometres.

DID YOU KNOW?

▶ An explosion at the Buncefield Oil Depot in Hertfordshire, UK, in 2005 (right) was caused by an overfilled fuel tank which allowed fuel to escape and clouds of vapour to form. Fuels are volatile liquids that evaporate into gases at room temperature. Fuel gas is very flammable and a small spark can start a fire. Once the fumes catch alight, the liquid fuel quickly follows. Smoking is not permitted at petrol stations for this very reason.

▶ A litre of any gas (at the same temperature and pressure) contains the same number of particles. This fact was discovered in the 1800s by Italian chemist, Amedeo Avogadro. Gases are very light, but a cubic metre of gas (such as air) contains billions of particles. In order to describe these large numbers, chemists use a measurement called the mole (or 'Avogadro's number'). During his studies, Avogadro found that 1 gram of hydrogen had the same number of particles as 12 grams of carbon. This was approximately 6.022×10^{23} particles (or one 'mole' of particles). One cubic metre of air is said to contain about 40 moles of particles.

4

The symbols of chemistry

In medieval times, the earliest chemists (alchemists) were the first to invent chemical symbols. When the alchemists carried out their experiments, they gave the substances they used (or produced) a small symbol so that they could easily communicate their results to others. Originally, the alchemists used the planets as symbols because, at the time, there was a close link between the study of the night sky and the study of the material world.

▲ Alchemists often worked in secret because they were regarded with suspicion. Their work, however, helped to lay the foundations of modern chemistry.

At first, the alchemists used symbols for metals – each with a distinct meaning. For example, gold was considered to be the most perfect of substances because it didn't react with anything. Gold was therefore given a symbol of a complete circle (rather like the Sun in shape and also golden yellow in colour). Silver was thought to

Metal	Planet symbol	Illustrated symbol
Gold	Sun	☉
Silver	Moon	☽
Mercury	Mercury	☿
Tin	Jupiter	♃
Lead	Saturn	♄
Copper	Venus	♀
Iron	Mars	♂

be nearly perfect, and given the symbol of a crescent Moon (not quite a complete and perfect circle. Silver also reflects a silvery light, rather like the Moon.). At the time, the alchemists were thought to be magicians because they could conjure up new substances. During times of medieval persecution, many alchemists were driven to invent their own secret symbols. Sometimes, cheats took over and **alchemy** became famous for its fraudulent practices.

MODERN SYMBOLS

In 1787, Lavoisier (see page 10) wrote a book naming all the chemical symbols that were known at the time. Then, in 1813, Swedish chemist Jöns Berzelius began to give each of these substances a symbol based on the first letter of its name. If elements began with the same letter, Berzelius added a second letter. For example, bismuth was given the symbol Bi and beryllium the symbol Be. Notice that when there are two letters in a chemical symbol, the first letter is always in upper case and the second letter in lower case.

Sometimes, chemical names originate from Latin. In these cases the chemical symbols are taken from the Latin (rather than the English) equivalent. For example:

Element	Latin name	Symbol
Iron	Ferrum	Fe
Silver	Argentum	Ag
Gold	Aurum	Au
Copper	Cuprum	Cu

Other elements have been named and given symbols based on their chemical or physical properties. For example, the term chlorine (Cl) comes from the Greek word chlôros (green). Bromine (Br) comes from the Greek word brômos (stench) because it has a strong smell.

Other elements have been named after places and people. For example, strontium (Sr) is named after a place in Scotland (Strontian). This element was first identified in rock material taken from a mine near Strontian. When uranium (U) was discovered, it was named in honour of the discovery of the planet Uranus eight years earlier. Einsteinium is named after the famous scientist Albert Einstein. We also have californium – discovered by a research group working at the University of California.

CHOOSING NAMES FOR NEW ELEMENTS

An international committee called IUPAC (International Union of Pure and Applied Chemistry) oversees the naming of new elements and compounds. When a new element is found, researchers have to formally propose a name for their discovery. These names are usually based on a myth or character, a mineral, a place, a property of the element, or a famous scientist. A proposed name is discussed by IUPAC before becoming internationally accepted. It is very important that we all understand what chemical symbols are so that chemists around the world can easily talk about the materials they work with.

In 1974, a dispute about the naming of element 104 was put to IUPAC. The element was discovered independently by two research groups – the Russian group wanted to call the element Dubnium (Db) whilst the Americans wanted to call it Rutherfordium (Rf) to honour the scientist Ernest Rutherford. IUPAC declared that the element 104 should be named Unnilquadium (from the Latin terms un (1), nil (0), quad (4) ium. This name was kept until 1997 when the matter was finally resolved and the element became Rutherfordium (Rf).

INVESTIGATE

▶ Research the names for these chemical symbols.

▶ Now find the chemical symbol for these elements.

(1) Na

(2) Mg

(3) Zn

(4) I

(5) Scandium

(6) Sulphur

(7) Antimony

(8) Lead

THE PERIODIC TABLE

We know that elements are basic materials that cannot be broken down into simpler substances but that combine to make the materials that we see around us. For example, the metal aluminium is an element made from only aluminium atoms. Oxygen is another element, but this time it is a gas made from only oxygen atoms. The different arrangement of particles in aluminium and oxygen atoms explains why these two elements have such contrasting properties.

One of the most important tools in chemistry is the **Periodic Table**. This table does more than just list all the known elements (currently about 111). The table has also been designed to group similar types of element together and gives flexibility to add more elements if they are discovered.

▲ Oxygen (top) is a colourless gas, while aluminium (left) is a solid metal. These elements have very different particle arrangements.

THE PERIODIC TABLE

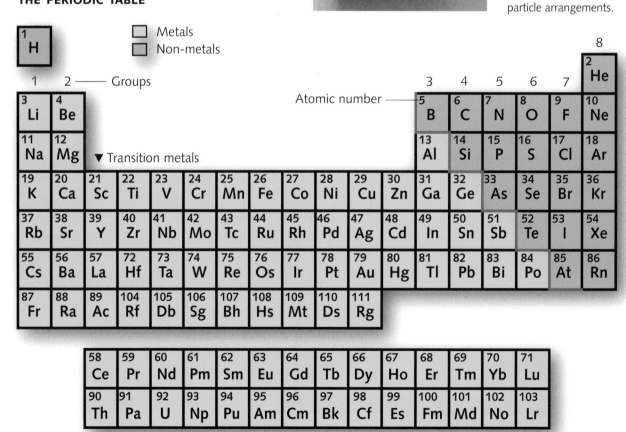

The Periodic Table contains some of the following features:

▶ Elements are organised into vertical columns (**groups**) and horizontal rows (**periods**). There are eight main groups organised around the central block, which is called the 'transition metals'. There are seven periods.

▶ If you look closely at some common elements you will notice they are broadly divided into metals and non-metals. As a rough guide, those on the right of the table are non-metals (for example, nitrogen, N) and those on the left are metallic (for example, magnesium, Mg). Now look at some elements you are not familiar with (such as selenium, Se). This is found on the right of the table so is likely to be a non-metal.

▶ The elements in the table are organised so that those in vertical groups contain elements with similar properties. If you look at the first group, for example, it contains the elements lithium (Li) and potassium (K). If you knew about the properties of lithium, you could predict that potassium is very similar before actually experimenting with this very reactive metal.

▶ The table is called 'periodic' because it arranges the elements in such a way that properties are repeated at fixed intervals. For example, if lithium (Li) has a particular property, as you move along the row, there are another eight elements before this property is seen again with sodium (Na) that sits below lithium. Another eight elements would lead us to potassium and hence the same property again. After this, the repeat interval increases to 18 elements, but the property remains periodic all the same.

INVESTIGATE

▶ Choose an element that is unknown to you from the Periodic Table, but is in the same group as one you are more familiar with. Make some predictions about the behaviour of your unknown element. Check your predictions using the internet. How useful a tool is the Periodic Table?

▶ Elements in the seventh row of the table contain atoms with a lot of protons and neutrons in their nucleus. These elements are radioactive. Their nucleus spontaneously disintegrates emitting high-energy particles. The elements are unstable because they don't have enough neutrons to balance the protons in the nucleus. If you bombard another atom with radioactive particles, some of the protons may be removed from the nucleus, altering the composition of the atom. You end up with a completely different element if the atomic structure of the nucleus changes.

DID YOU KNOW?

▶ Six elements make up nearly all (99 per cent) of your mass and the atoms in your body – calcium, hydrogen, carbon, phosphorous, oxygen and nitrogen. The body also contains a selection of many other elements in small amounts, such as potassium, sulphur, sodium and magnesium. We help to replenish our body with these important substances by eating a balanced diet. Two-thirds of the body is composed of water so hydrogen and oxygen are the most common elements in the body.

▶ In 1980, Dr Glenn Seaborg managed to change a few thousand atoms of lead into gold using a nuclear reactor. Seaborg used high-energy particles to split the nuclei of lead atoms so that they released three protons. Gold has three protons less than lead (79 compared to 82) enabling Seaborg to successfully create this precious element. However, Seaborg's experiment needed an enormous amount of energy so this form of gold would be far too expensive to produce commercially.

TIME TRAVEL: DEVELOPING THE PERIODIC TABLE

The modern Periodic Table is the result of the genius work of a number of prominent scientists. The Periodic Table is not a regular-shaped table as we might expect, but one that has a unique structure and order that can only have been derived from observations of the few elements that were known at the time. The actual shape of today's table is similar to that first proposed, but was finally agreed by an international committee in 1985 after years of discussion. The format of the Periodic Table means that new elements can be added at any time. Chemists also use 'ingredients' from the Periodic Table to build molecules that have never existed on Earth before.

Since the first element was discovered, scientists have been classifying elements according to their properties. At first this was simply a case of comparing metals with gases, but as more and more elements were discovered, basic classification became more difficult.

ATTEMPTING TO CLASSIFY THE ELEMENTS

▶ In 1829, a German scientist named Johann Döbereiner announced his 'Law of Triads' in an attempt to classify the elements more precisely. This law put elements into groups of three that had similar chemical properties. This meant that the properties of the middle element could be predicted from the two elements on either side.

▶ The ideas of Döbereiner were extended in 1843 when German chemist Leopold Gmelin published his work. Gmelin also grouped elements together, but he used three groups of four elements and one group of five – the latter included nitrogen and phosphorus (and became the fifth group of the modern Periodic Table).

▶ Groups of three, four or five elements were the limit to progress at this time because scientists had yet to discover the atomic mass (see page 12) – a property common to all elements. The atomic mass was discovered by Italian chemist Stanislao Cannizzaro in 1858. Although scientists couldn't weigh individual atoms, they had discovered a way of using electricity to split molecules into individual atoms so that they could be compared. Cannizzaro gave hydrogen a value of 'one' and assigned an 'atomic mass' to the other elements in comparison.

▶ In 1865, English scientist John Newlands came close to the modern Periodic Table by suggesting the 'Law of Octaves'. Newlands recognised that there were repeated chemical patterns after every eight elements, but was not secure in his chemical knowledge to order the elements in their current irregular structure. Newlands' table also did not leave any gaps to account for the discovery of additional elements – a major downfall of his theory.

▼ Part of Newlands' table (below). The table had repeating patterns but the metal iron (Fe) was in the same group as two non-metals, oxygen (O) and sulphur (S).

H	Li	Be	B	C	N	O
F	Na	Mg	Al	Si	P	S
Cl	K	Ca	Cr	Ti	Mn	Fe

Dimitri Mendeleev

In February 1869, a Russian chemist called Dimitri Mendeleev wrote each element and its chief properties on separate cards and began to lay them out in various patterns. Mendeleev put the lightest element (hydrogen) in the top left corner and the heaviest atom in the bottom right corner. He then began a new line every time he came to an element that had properties similar to hydrogen. The pattern that he finally settled upon had similar elements grouped in vertical columns, unlike his first table, which grouped them horizontally.

The layout of Mendeleev's table brought some interesting discoveries:

(1) Gaps were left for missing elements.

Mendeleev was confident about his arrangement of elements so he left gaps for undiscovered elements (but also used surrounding elements to predict the properties of undiscovered elements). For example, he predicted the properties of three unknown elements and within six years, scandium, gallium and germanium were discovered. His most famous example was gallium. Mendeleev predicted that gallium had a density of 5.9g cm^{-3}. Gallium was discovered in 1875. Later, its **density** was measured as 5.956 g cm^{-3} – matching Mendeleev's estimation.

(2) Some elements were originally placed in the Periodic Table in the incorrect groups.

At the time, beryllium oxide (an oxide of the element beryllium) was reported as having the chemical formula Be_2O_3. This would have put beryllium in group three of Mendeleev's table. However, with no space in this group, Mendeleev placed beryllium in the second group because it matched these properties. In fact, much later, scientists discovered that beryllium oxide actually had the formula BeO. Mendeleev had correctly placed beryllium in group two.

(3) Some elements were originally placed in the table in the wrong order according to their atomic mass.

For example, Mendeleev placed tellurium (Te) before iodine (I) even though their atomic masses were the other way around. Mendeleev did this because their

▲ Although other chemists had recognised patterns in the properties of elements, Dimitri Mendeleev was the first to realise the significance of these patterns.

respective chemical properties matched the rest of the groups correctly. Mendeleev presumed that the mass of tellurium had been incorrectly calculated. The mass was in fact correct, but many years later, scientists discovered another atom of tellurium that had a different atomic mass – and was heavier than iodine! This phenomenon has been repeated with three more pairs of elements in the Periodic Table, following the discovery of new elements (see Investigate exercise).

Investigate

▶ When Mendeleev's table was created, only 65 elements were known. Today, the Periodic Table contains 111 elements. In addition to tellurium and iodine, there are three more pairs of elements that have been arranged in the incorrect order of atomic mass. Can you find what they are using the internet?

5

Discovering the elements

When Mendeleev first put his Periodic Table together in 1869, 65 elements were known. During the remainder of his lifetime another 14 elements were discovered giving Mendeleev the satisfaction of knowing that his predictions were largely correct. Following his death in 1907, eight more elements were discovered and 24 were created artificially in laboratory conditions. The majority of these new elements are the very heavy ones that we find at the bottom of the Periodic Table.

▶ Lead

ALCHEMY

Alchemy is considered to be the ancestor of chemistry — an art that was handed down through the centuries. Alchemy was born in ancient Egypt (Al-chemia is an Arab name which means 'to pour or cast together'). The practice quickly spread through Spain and the rest of Europe and was also developed in China. The alchemists were fascinated by the elements. In particular, they spent much of their time in search of the philosopher's stone. The alchemists thought this unknown substance had the power to turn lead into gold and held the secret of eternal youth and good health.

◀ Tin

▼ Mercury

OTHER ANCIENT ELEMENTS

The alchemists experimented with substances by heating and mixing them together. They found some of the elements, such as iron, mercury, tin, lead, silver, gold and copper. However, other elements present at the time remained undiscovered for many years because they were inaccessible. For example, the alchemists did not discover hydrogen because in its pure form, it is a colourless, odourless gas that is not easy to detect. Hydrogen is mainly found combined with oxygen in the form of water. Hydrogen was eventually discovered in 1766 by the English chemist Henry Cavendish. When Cavendish experimented with acids and mercury he found that these substances reacted to produce hydrogen gas.

▼ Gold

▼ Coins containing copper

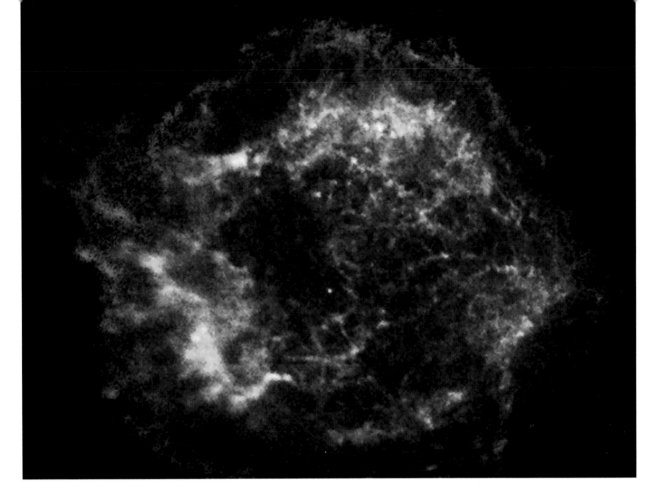

HIDDEN ELEMENTS

Some elements arise from the behaviour of other elements. For example, when hydrogen atoms collide at high speed, they stick together and form heavier atoms of the element helium. This process is called '**fusion**' and forms the basis of every star that we see in the night sky. Stars are made of hydrogen gas that is pulled together by the force of gravity. In the smallest stars, hydrogen fuses together to form helium. In medium-sized stars, helium fuses together to form oxygen and carbon, and in larger stars, heavier elements such as neon, sodium, sulphur and iron are formed.

Elements heavier than iron cannot be made in a star through the process of fusion. Instead, these heavier atoms are made in a gigantic explosion (called a supernova) at the end of the life of a very large star (called a blue giant). Astronomers have studied supernovae and stars to see the elements

▲ During a supernova, elements heavier than iron are made and scattered into the Universe.

that they contain using a technique called spectroscopy. Spectroscopy detects the emission of light rays and other electromagnetic particles. Many elements have been discovered in space using spectroscopy, including some very reactive elements, such as caesium and rubidium.

THE SEARCH FOR UN-REACTIVE ELEMENTS

Un-reactive elements were more difficult to find. For example, argon (a colourless, odourless and very un-reactive gas) was only discovered in 1894 when English chemists William Ramsay and Lord Rayleigh experimented with liquefied air. They discovered that a mystery element (named argon) accounted for about one per cent of air. Their finding soon led to the discovery of other inert gases (found on the right of the Periodic Table).

FINDING VERY REACTIVE ELEMENTS

Many of our most reactive metals combine tightly with other elements in our Earth's crust and are very difficult to find and extract. For example, aluminium metal was not discovered until 1825. Aluminium can only be extracted from its ore by the use of electricity (which was not fully developed until the 1800s).

FINDING ELEMENTS USING RADIOACTIVITY

Radioactivity is a process caused by the nucleus of certain atoms breaking down and emitting smaller particles (see page 25). This process has occurred for billions of years. However, some radioactive elements were not discovered until 1898 – when Pierre and Marie Curie identified radium and polonium, for example. At the time, the phenomenon of radioactivity had been recently discovered in uranium ore. However, when extracting uranium from its ore, the Curies noticed that the waste material was also radioactive, suggesting the presence of other elements.

◀ Pierre and Marie Curie extracted the radioactive elements radium and polonium from uranium ore.

MAKING ELEMENTS

The last 24 elements of the Periodic Table have been created in the laboratory, rather than discovered as natural elements on Earth.

INVESTIGATE

▶ Examine the Periodic Table and pick an element you do not know. Research how this element was discovered. Was it discovered using electricity, radioactivity, spectroscopy or some other means?

Although synthetic, these are still considered to be elements because they are composed of just one type of atom. One of the difficulties in making new elements is that the nuclei are so heavy that they are unstable (and therefore short-lived). These elements are usually made by bombarding other elements with atoms (or parts of atoms). An example of a synthetic element is curium. This element was produced in 1994 by scientists in America. It is named after the Curies and is now used in satellite technology.

DID YOU KNOW?

▶ The Sun is a star, but it is too small to form a supernova (only stars that are at least eight times bigger than our Sun end their lives in this way). Luckily for us, the Sun will not explode. However, stars lose some of their matter as energy during the process of fusion – the Sun has already used up about half of its hydrogen, and in another five billion years the Sun's hydrogen will have been used up completely. At this time, the Sun will expand to form what astronomers call a 'red giant', swallowing up planets, such as Mercury, Venus and eventually the Earth. The Sun will then cool, shrink and fade away.

▶ American scientist, Dr Glenn Seaborg (1912-1999) contributed to the discovery of ten elements in the Periodic Table – a contribution to chemistry far beyond that expected from just one person. Seaborg discovered plutonium and co-discovered another element, seaborgium, which is named after him. Seaborg also discovered almost 100 different forms of already known elements (which we call isotopes).

Changing physical states

6

Gases, liquids and solids have very different properties because their particles are arranged in different ways. To change from one physical state to another, heat energy is usually required. If you take an ice cube from the freezer, for example, it will eventually turn into a small pool of water at room temperature. The heat from the room has caused the solid water (ice) to turn into liquid water. Heating the pool of water further would cause it to evaporate and finally boil into a gas (steam). Pressure can also be used to change a substance from one physical state into another.

CHANGING BETWEEN LIQUIDS AND GASES

LIQUID TO GAS

When it rains, puddles form that are mostly liquid water. The Sun dries these puddles gradually. As the Sun shines, the warmth heats the particles in the puddle so that they gain more energy. This gain in energy causes the particles to vibrate a little more so that they break free from the intermolecular forces of attraction between particles. Eventually, the particles break away from each other. When particles overcome the forces of attraction, they escape from the liquid – this is called evaporation.

When all the particles break their forces of attraction, the substance turns into a gas, and we call this **boiling**. The temperature of the boiling point can be affected by a number of conditions, such as the presence of other substances in the liquid or the altitude at which the water is being heated. Boiling points are very precise for pure liquids and are often used as a means of identifying substances. For example, in its pure form, water will boil at 100°C (at one atmosphere pressure).

If you boil a kettle on the top of a mountain you may find that the kettle boils at a lower temperature. At high altitudes, the air is described as 'thin' because there are fewer air particles present and the air pressure is lower than at sea-level. When the water is heated, there are fewer particles in the air to prevent the water particles from escaping.

▲ The boiling point of water changes with varying altitude. At high altitude you can make tea very quickly – but it won't be as tasty because water at a lower temperature is less efficient at leaching out the tea!

GASES TO LIQUIDS

When gases are cooled, the molecules lose some of their energy, they move more slowly, and the gas 'condenses'. As the particles lose energy they move closer together and the forces of attraction begin to restrict their movement so that they become liquid. **Condensation** can be observed in cold weather – if we breathe onto a pane of cold glass, our warm breath condenses as the water vapour cools. Gases also form liquids, in a similar way, when they are compressed (see page 21).

▲ Solid iodine sublimes (see below) at room temperature.

CHANGING BETWEEN SOLIDS AND GASES

Solids can also be converted straight into gases (and vice versa) without a liquid stage in-between. This process is called **sublimation** and is quite rare. 'Stage smoke' uses the principle of sublimation. It is made from frozen carbon dioxide gas (called 'dry ice') that sublimes to form a smoky effect. While these physical changes are taking place, the amount of substance does not change – it just changes from one physical state into another.

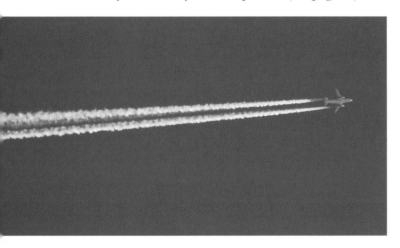

▲ The vapour trail following an aeroplane is partly formed by steam from the exhaust condensing into water droplets and ice crystals when it is cooled by the air.

CHANGING BETWEEN LIQUIDS AND SOLIDS

LIQUIDS TO SOLIDS

Freezing occurs when a liquid changes into a solid. If liquid particles are cooled they begin to form a regular structure. As they lose energy, the particles are less able to move apart.

SOLIDS TO LIQUIDS

When solids gain heat energy, the particles vibrate more vigorously and can break the forces holding them together. The particles begin to behave like a liquid and **melting** occurs. The 'melting point' can tell us a lot about the identity of a pure substance.

DID YOU KNOW?

▶ When water freezes, its volume increases. The same number of particles occupy more space which is why ice is less dense than water. This phenomenon can cause problems at home in the winter. During cold weather, water in pipes can freeze and expand – and if the pipes burst, the water can flood a home. Using insulation around the pipes helps to keep them warm enough to prevent this from happening.

▶ The water under the Arctic ice is close to freezing but some fish have adapted to survive there. They produce a molecule in their blood that is very similar to the anti-freeze that people put into car radiators. This helps the fish to survive in conditions that would freeze other creatures to death.

▶ The explosive chosen by the terrorists who attempted to attack the London Underground system on 21 July 2005, failed to detonate. Experts believe this was because the explosive was a substance that sublimes at room temperature.

A CLOSER LOOK AT PHYSICAL CHANGES

The three states of matter (solids, liquids and gases) can be changed by any one physical change. These are summarised by the triangle below.

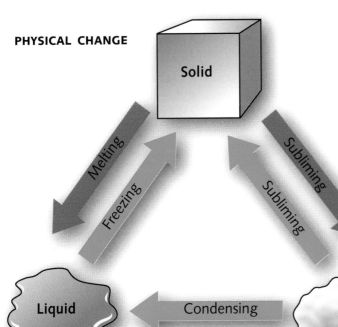

PHYSICAL CHANGE

DIFFERENT TYPES OF SOLID

Although the particles in a solid are held tightly together, variations in these patterns can explain why some solids float whilst others sink. Compare the behaviour of a piece of metal with a piece of plastic, when put into a large tank of water. It would not be unreasonable to assume that the piece of metal would sink whilst the piece of plastic would float. This is because metal and plastic have different densities.

In metals, the particles are held very tightly together with very few spaces between them. This tight structure means that a greater number of metal particles are packed into one area and the material is described as dense. Dense solids will sink in water because their density is greater than that of the water. The particles in plastics are also held tightly together making the material a solid. However, the rows of particles have gaps between them. This means that plastic has a lower density than metal. Plastic will float in water if its density is lower than that of the water.

HEATING SOLIDS

Most solids **expand**, just before they reach their melting point and turn into a liquid. This is because the particles start to move apart as the forces of attraction become weaker. Some metal bridges have small gaps between the metal parts. On hot days, the metal particles can vibrate a little more than usual and this causes a slight expansion to occur. In order to maintain the shape and structure of the bridge, small gaps are left to allow for this natural movement. When the weather cools again, the metal **contracts**.

33

HEATING GASES

Like solids, gases can also expand and contract. The particles in hot gases have more energy than in cold gases and as they move about more vigorously they occupy a greater volume. This can have useful applications. For example, a blast of hot air that is less dense than the surrounding air can lift a hot air balloon.

GAS PRESSURE

Gas particles move randomly and they bounce off each other and the sides of the container in which they are stored. Each time a particle rebounds with the container it exerts a small pressure – caused by energy from the particle being transferred to the wall of the container. Gas pressure can be increased in the following ways:

▶ **Increasing temperature**. This gives the gas particles more energy and therefore increases both the frequency and the energy of each collision. Gas pressure will increase at higher temperatures.

▶ **Decreasing volume/increasing pressure**. If a gas is compressed, the same number of gas particles occupy a smaller space. This means that the frequency of collisions (and therefore the pressure) will be increased. If a gas is compressed very quickly, its temperature is also raised (which adds to the increasing pressure).

▲ The gas in a hot air balloon cools as the balloon moves higher. If the volume decreases, the balloon will sink again.

TEST YOURSELF

▶ Why do balloons burst if you keep blowing air into them?
▶ If a gas is transferred from a small container to a larger one, what happens to the pressure?

Mixtures and compounds

7

When elements are combined together, they form either a mixture or a compound. Compounds are formed by chemical reactions that usually require heat energy. For example, if the elements iron and sulphur are combined together without heating, we have a mixture of iron and sulphur. However, if these two elements are combined and heated, we form a compound called iron sulphide.

MIXTURES VS COMPOUNDS

A mixture is two or more elements mixed together (which could be separated again by physical means). A mixture can be compared to a sample of red and blue counters. We can clearly see the properties of the counters and can easily separate them. In contrast, a compound is two or more elements chemically combined together. A compound is formed when the atoms of various elements donate, receive or share electrons with each other to form molecules. This is called chemical bonding (see page 15).

A mixture displays the same properties as the individual elements from which it is made. In contrast, a compound has new properties of its own. For example, an iron and sulphur mixture looks like a combination of yellow and grey powders but can easily be separated using a magnet. In contrast, iron sulphide has a completely new appearance (a black solid) and is not magnetic. Iron sulphide can only be separated using another chemical process that breaks the newly-formed bonds. This is because the iron has donated some of its outermost electrons to the sulphur to form a chemical compound.

TYPES OF MIXTURES

SOLID/SOLID MIXTURES

Mixtures of this kind are made from different solids. Sand and soil are two examples. Soil is made up of different types of particles and sand contains small sand particles as well as parts of shells and larger pebbles. These examples are mixtures because heat was not involved in their formation and the particles can easily be separated.

▼ A mixture of iron and sulphur can be separated using a magnet because the iron is attracted towards the magnetic force.

SOLID/LIQUID MIXTURES

When it rains heavily, soil can mix with the rainwater to form a muddy liquid. This is also a mixture because no heat is involved and no chemical reactions have taken place. If you look closely at a muddy puddle you may see small particles of soil floating around. This is called a suspension. The soil particles can be easily separated from the water.

SOLID/GAS MIXTURES

Solids and gases can also form mixtures. Sometimes, the exterior walls of houses or buildings are cleaned up using a sand-blasting technique. The dust that comes off the walls is very fine and mixes with the surrounding air. If left, this dust will eventually settle and become separated from the air again. A similar observation is made when a car drives down a dusty road. Dust from the road is scattered into the air creating a mixture. Nature also provides us with examples of solid/gas mixtures. During volcanic eruptions, for example, the exploding flow of ash and rock is a highly dangerous hot mixture of solid and gas material.

LIQUID/LIQUID AND LIQUID/GAS MIXTURES

What happens when we make a drink of orange squash by mixing concentrated orange squash with water? We make a mixture from these two liquids. This process doesn't involve heat, no chemical bonds have formed, and the two liquids can be separated from each other. Fizzy drinks, such as lemonade, are examples of liquid/gas mixtures. To make these drinks fizzy, manufacturers inject carbon dioxide gas through the liquid. The liquid and gas can be separated again by leaving the lid off the bottle. It may take a few days, but eventually the drink turns 'flat'.

TYPES OF COMPOUNDS

Compounds, like mixtures, are made up from at least two different elements. However, unlike mixtures, compounds are formed when energy causes a chemical reaction. This energy is usually heat, but chemists also use electricity, light or even the energy stored in other chemicals. A chemical reaction forces the elements to bond together by rearranging their electrons to create more stable products. This makes them difficult to separate.

◀ A volcanic eruption can throw millions of tonnes of ash into the air.

Compounds display completely new properties. For example, water is a colourless liquid made from the elements hydrogen and oxygen – both colourless and odourless gases. Compounds differ from mixtures because they:

▶ Need a chemical reaction to form.
▶ Can only be separated by using another chemical reaction.
▶ Do not necessarily have the same properties as their constituent elements.
▶ Contain the constituent elements in definite proportions. Therefore, water always contains twice as much hydrogen as oxygen (H_2O).

NON-METAL BONDING

Elements bond in a number of different ways. Non-metals bond by sharing electrons. Atoms will try to maximise the number of electrons in their outer shells when they bond (see page 15) and the best way for non-metals to do this is by sharing electrons. For example, water (H_2O) has two hydrogen atoms and one oxygen atom. Oxygen has six electrons in its outer (second) shell and to achieve the full complement of eight, it shares two electrons with a hydrogen atom. This is called covalent bonding.

METAL AND NON-METAL BONDING

A metal and a non-metal will bond together by donating and receiving electrons. Salt, for example, is a compound of sodium and chlorine. Sodium has one electron in its outer shell and chlorine has seven. However, both of these atoms can gain the full complement of electrons on their outer shell if sodium gives its 'spare' electron to chlorine. This is called ionic bonding.

NAMING COMPOUNDS

There is no systematic way of naming compounds made from two non-metallic elements – many of the names simply have to be learnt. To make things simpler, chemists around the world use formulae for the compounds they are working with. This creates a communal language between all scientists. The table (below) shows some common compounds with their names and formulae.

Hydrogen chloride	HCl
Water	H_2O
Carbon monoxide	CO
Carbon dioxide	CO_2
Ammonia	NH_3
Ammonium chloride	NH_4Cl
Hydrochloric acid	HCl
Sulphuric acid	H_2SO_4
Nitric acid	HNO_3
Methane	CH_4

COMPOUNDS FROM METALS AND NON-METALS

When atoms have gained or lost electrons they become charged. Certain atoms will always form the same charge. Aluminium, for example, always loses three electrons when it forms a compound and we say that it has a 3+ charge. Compounds that are formed from these charged atoms are called **ions**. Some common ions are shown in the table below.

Charge 3+	Charge 2+	Charge 1+	Charge 1-	Charge 2-
(aluminium) Al^{3+}	(magnesium) Mg^{2+}	(hydrogen) H^+	(hydroxide) OH^-	(oxide) O^{2-}
(chromium) Cr^{3+}	(calcium) Ca^{2+}	(sodium) Na^+	(chloride) Cl^-	(sulphide) S^{2-}
(iron) Fe^{3+}	(copper) Cu^{2+}	(lithium) Li^+	(iodide) I^-	(sulphate) SO_4^{2-}

When ions are combined together we use a technique called 'swap and drop' to determine the formula of the new compound. Swap and drop is conducted in the following way:

▶ Write down the symbol for each of the ions involved and their charges beneath them. For example, a compound of hydrogen and sulphide would be written as:

H S

1 2

▶ Swap and drop these numbers as shown below.

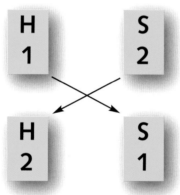

▶ The numbers in the second row tell us that the formula has two hydrogen (H) atoms and one sulphide (S) atom. This is written as H_2S. The name for this compound is hydrogen sulphide – a combination of the two names.

TEST YOURSELF

▶ Using the swap and drop technique, work out the formula and name for each of the following combinations of ions.

1. Sodium and hydroxide

2. Magnesium and chloride

3. Calcium and oxide

UNEXPECTED DISCOVERIES

Sometimes, during their laboratory work, scientists make new discoveries about some very useful compounds. The following historical examples introduced some of the compounds that we commonly use today.

DYES

In 1856, a chemist's assistant called William Perkin was given the task of artificially preparing an anti-malarial drug called quinine whilst working during his college holidays. At the time Perkin was just 18 years old and had little laboratory experience. He was working with a product made from coal tar but instead of producing quinine, he created a mysterious black substance. Thankfully, Perkin's curiosity led him to explore the substance further. He dissolved it in alcohol and found that it produced a stunning purple-coloured solution. Perkin then discovered that the purple solution dyed fabrics, such as silk and cotton, and did not wash out or fade in the Sun. In fact, Perkin had discovered a mauve dye (called mauveine).

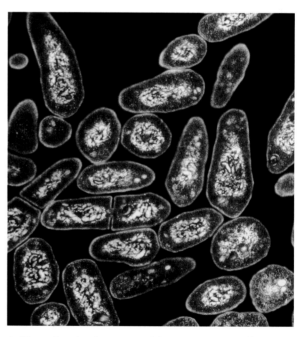

▲ Mauveine dye is now used in microscopy work to colour bacteria, such as cholera or tuberculosis (above).

Other dyes were also discovered by accident. In 1928, a blue dye was isolated at a chemical plant in Scotland. A worker called Dandridge noticed that blue crystals were forming on the inside of a sealed container during the industrial process. The crystals were produced when iron in the container reacted with substances to create a by-product called phthalocyanine. At the time, phthalocyanine was not given much attention, but 20 years later it was found that when copper combined with phthalocyanine, it created a rich blue colour. This led to the discovery of a blue dye called 'monastral blue' which is now used in paints and printing inks. The dye is the pigment used to dye the British £5 note.

NYLON

In 1930, a team of American chemists, led by Dr Wallace Carothers at the chemicals and healthcare company DuPont, were trying to unravel natural fibres of rubber and silk to discover the composition of these useful materials. The researchers hoped they could copy the properties for other synthetic materials, such as polyesters.

One afternoon when Carothers was out of the laboratory, the young chemists had some fun to see how far they could pull a fibre from the polyester solution. They were surprised to find that a fibre was produced as long as the corridor and they quickly realised that they were on the verge of making an important discovery.

Polyesters have very low melting points making them difficult to make into fabrics. The scientists therefore decided to repeat the experiment on another group of man-made materials called polyamides. And this was how nylon was discovered! Nylon is a very successful clothing

▶ Nylon is a synthetic fibre discovered in the 1930s. It is now used to make fabrics, ropes and some medical products.

product. When nylon stockings went on sale in New York in 1940, over four million pairs were sold in a few hours.

SILK

Silk is a natural fibre farmed from the cocoons of silk worm caterpillars. During the 1870s, French scientist Louis Pasteur was asked to help investigate a disease that killed silk worms, threatening to ruin the French silk industry. Pasteur's young assistant Chardonnet accidentally spilled a substance in the laboratory but didn't clean up the mess until sometime later. On his return, he discovered that the substance had turned fibrous and resembled the structure of silk. Chardonnet experimented further and discovered the compound rayon.

INVESTIGATE

▶ Research the discovery of penicillin by Alexander Fleming with the following questions in mind.

1. How far was the discovery due to luck?

2. How has Fleming's discovery been used today? What have its disadvantages been?

3. What aspects of Fleming's discovery have we developed?

Compounds are all around us and can be found as solids, liquids or gases. We have found many useful roles for everyday compounds. However, despite the wealth of materials already at our disposal, chemists are always on the look out for new materials that could be used in our daily lives.

SYNTHETIC DIAMONDS

Diamond is a very precious mineral that is difficult to find. It is made from the element carbon that becomes heated under great pressure, hundreds of kilometres below the Earth's surface, during the Earth's natural geological cycle.

In recent years, chemists have successfully recreated these conditions in a laboratory to make diamonds of their own. The first synthetic diamond was made in 1954 when scientists subjected graphite to extreme

temperature and pressure conditions. The experiment, however, needed so much electricity that it was cheaper to buy an actual diamond! Today, synthetic diamonds can be made more cheaply. They can be used for jewellery (left) but are also used extensively in industry, to make long-lasting cutting tools. Synthetic diamonds are also a useful material for the microelectronics industry – they are extremely hard-wearing and can be shaped into minute pieces, without breaking.

SELF-CLEANING WINDOWS

A compound called titanium dioxide (TiO_2) has been developed by a team of researchers at the University of Texas, USA, to create self-cleaning windows. When sunlight hits the titanium dioxide coating, the electrons gain energy and move away from the titanium dioxide compound. This in turn creates what we call **free radicals** that react with dirt on the window making it clean, and also prevent the glass from fogging. Self-cleaning glass is not on the market at present, but the technology has enormous potential.

NON-STICKING PLASTICS

Scientists at the Dow Chemical Company, USA, have developed a non-stick coating that cannot be written on and that repels water and other liquids. The plastic is mostly composed of carbon, but combined with atoms of the element fluorine. The fluorine atoms are positioned on the outside of the plastic and it is these that resist substances sticking to them. The company is researching possible uses of their new plastic in hospitals, on kitchen and bathroom surfaces, and as a potential material for aircraft wings (making the wings easier to de-ice). The plastic could also be used in artificial heart valves to prevent the formation of blood clots. At present, however, the plastic is damaged by high temperatures – and therefore cannot be used in some cooking utensils.

▲ A non-sticking plastic coating on this wall could prevent it from becoming covered with graffiti.

DID YOU KNOW?

▶ A company in Chicago, USA, charges $4,000 to $22,000 to turn the ashes of your loved ones into synthetic diamonds from their carbon remains. The process has taken three years to perfect, but involves the purification of cremation ashes at temperatures of 3,000°C, followed by further heating and pressure. This forms a diamond after 16 weeks. The longer the process is carried out, the higher the quality of diamond achieved.

Separating mixtures

8

Mixtures are created when two or more elements are combined together in the absence of a chemical reaction. Unlike compounds, mixtures can be separated using a variety of simple techniques. Two common separation techniques used by chemists today are called evaporation and **distillation**.

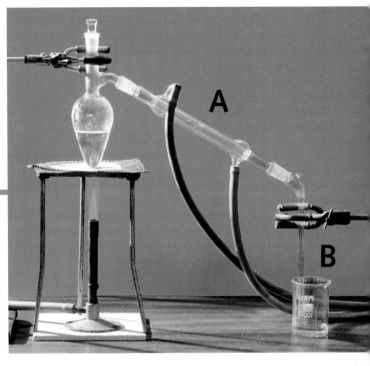

▲ Distillation equipment can be used to separate mixtures that have different boiling points.

EVAPORATION

When a solid is dissolved in water, the two parts can be separated using evaporation if we want to retain the solid component. Seawater, for example, has salt dissolved in it. If the seawater is heated so that the water boils away, a white residue is left behind which can be tested and proven to be salt. If you swim in the sea and allow your skin to dry in the Sun, you may find white deposits on your skin. These are salt deposits from the seawater.

DISTILLATION

If we want to retain both parts of the solution, chemists use the process of distillation. Distillation can also be used to separate two liquids. Soft drinks are mixtures that can be separated using distillation equipment like that shown above. If the mixture is heated, the parts with the lowest boiling points will boil first and leave the liquid mixture as a gas. The vapours will travel to the condenser at the top (A) and condense into a liquid as they are cooled. The condensed liquid will then travel to the collecting flask (B). Distillation equipment has the following features that enable liquids to become separated:

▶ The condenser is surrounded by a cold water jacket, connected to a tap. Cold water is constantly flowing from the bottom of the condenser towards the top. This means that the condenser is never warmed by the rising hot vapours and will always remain cold.

▶ The heated end of the equipment is usually held higher than the collecting end so that gravity can help the condensed vapours to flow into the collecting vessel.

▶ Sometimes, a thermometer is used to indicate the boiling point of the component that has evaporated. This is useful for identification purposes. In the simple distillation of cola, for example, the component that boils off first (called the distillate) has a boiling point of 100°C and is identified as water.

INDUSTRIAL SEPARATION PROCESSES

Many of the products we use in everyday life come from crude oil – the remains of ancient plants and animals found deep beneath the Earth's surface. The oil formed when these remains became buried, squashed and heated over millions of years. The term 'crude' means a mixture – crude oil is a mixture of many useful components. However, it is not possible to separate these using simple distillation. Instead, crude oil is separated using a process called **fractional distillation**.

SEPARATING CRUDE OIL

The equipment needed for fractional distillation is similar to that of simple distillation – both involve heating to boil off components and collecting the vapours for condensing. We call each component that is extracted a 'fraction'.

During fractional distillation, crude oil is passed through the bottom of a column and heated slowly. The fractions of the oil with the lowest boiling points evaporate first and travel to the top of the column where it is cooler. Here, they condense and are collected on small trays, to prevent them from falling to the bottom of the column again. The condensing process slightly heats this top area of the column.

Meanwhile, the remainder of the crude oil is heated further so that the next lowest boiling fraction evaporates. This vapour travels to the point near to the top of the column where it is coolest (just below the first fraction) and condensation and collection occur again. This process continues until eight different fractions of oil have been collected.

REFINING CRUDE OIL

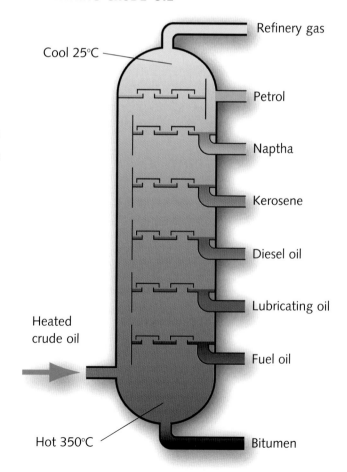

Cool 25°C

Refinery gas

Petrol

Naptha

Kerosene

Diesel oil

Lubricating oil

Heated crude oil

Fuel oil

Hot 350°C

Bitumen

At the end of distillation, the fractionating column is cooler at the top than at the bottom. This is because those fractions condensing at the bottom have the highest boiling points and as they condense they release some of their heat. The process of separating oil by distillation is called refining.

The fractions of crude oil are summarised below:

Fraction	Boiling temperature (°C)	Amount produced (%)	Use
Refinery gas	< 25	2.1	Fuels
Petrol	40 - 75	31	Car fuel
Naptha	75 - 150	4	Chemicals
Kerosene	150 - 240	10.6	Aviation fuel
Diesel oil	220 - 250	30.2	Diesel engine vehicles
Lubricating oil	250- 350	1.7	Machine oil
Fuel oil	250 - 350	18	Industrial heating
Bitumen	> 350	2.4	Road tar

of these higher boiling fractions by a process called cracking. At an oil refinery, much of the work involves making the crude oil into as many useful and clean products for commercial use, as possible.

CRUDE OIL – SOME FACTS

The demands that we have on crude oil mean that its distillation is a continuous process. The different proportions of fractions produced can affect the price of the products they make. In 2004, in the United States, for example, there were approximately 21 million barrels of crude oil extracted that year, but this was down nine per cent on the previous year (2003). In fact, statistics show that supplies of extractable crude oil reserves are falling each year.

The amount of these fractions produced depends on the natural forces that formed the oil in the first place (and where the oil is therefore extracted). For example, North Sea oil produces about six per cent petrol and 19 per cent diesel oil. Some South American crude oils have only ten per cent diesel oil and the remainder are the fractions that boil at higher temperatures. Fuel companies have now developed ways in which they can make more useful fractions from some of the other oil products. For example, petrol can be made from some

DID YOU KNOW?

▶ Sometimes, materials decompose when they are subjected to high temperatures, making it difficult to separate them from each other. These mixtures can be distilled using a technique called vacuum distillation. A pump is used to reduce some of the air pressure in the equipment so that the liquids boil at lower temperatures (see page 31) making the mixtures less likely to decompose.

▶ Scientists have discovered ways to convert coal into oil. Oil reserves are running out quickly and using large coal reserves to make oil would be a good alternative source of fuel while alternative energy sources are still being researched. The coal is converted using a technique called the 'Fischer-Tropsch process'. In South Africa, for example, the company Sasol use this technique to produce most of the country's diesel fuel from coal.

CHROMATOGRAPHY

Some mixtures, such as ink, can be separated by a technique called **chromatography**. Chromatography can take a number of different forms but all have certain features in common. All types of chromatography need a substance to act as a solvent to dissolve the mixture that is being separated. The technique also requires a surface through which the dissolved mixture can travel. In the case of simple chromatography, this surface is paper.

SEPARATING INK

The ink that people use in their fountain pens is actually a mixture of different coloured pigments that give the ink its final colour. If you use a fountain pen, you may already realise the importance of not getting the page wet – the ink 'runs' and the writing becomes smudged. Fountain pen ink dissolves in water – the solvent that can be used in this type of chromatography.

▲ Black ink dissolves in water and can smudge if it becomes wet.

Chromatography works by the principle that the components of a mixture dissolve in a solvent to different extents (and are retained to a greater or lesser extent by the surface through which they are travelling). Some components are very soluble and will stay in the solution for longer than less soluble components. As the dissolved mixture travels through the material, the components are deposited at different lengths and the mixture becomes separated. If paper is used, a streak appears on its surface with varying colours. The results of chromatography are called chromatograms. The following experiment can be used to separate the colours of ink:

(1) Draw a line in pencil just above the bottom of a strip of filter paper. This marks the position of the ink so we can measure how far the different components have travelled, using a ruler. The line must be drawn with a pencil because other types of ink may interfere with the process.

(2) Drop a small spot of ink onto the pencil line.

(3) Place the filter paper into a beaker of water so that the water line falls just below the pencil line. The water molecules are attracted to the absorbent filter paper and are pulled up in a stream. When the first molecules leave the water, the next molecules follow because they are attracted to the paper (this is called capillary action). The chromatography is completed when the water stops moving, or has reached the top of the paper.

CHROMATOGRAM

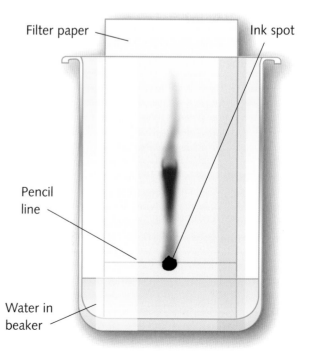

Filter paper

Ink spot

Pencil line

Water in beaker

OTHER TYPES OF CHROMATOGRAPHY

Chemists often use chromatography to identify the components present in mixtures to see how pure they are. Sometimes, forensic scientists use the same principles to match substances from crime scenes, such as paint pigments or drugs. In recent years, chromatography has developed with the aid of computer technology. This enables scientists to separate complex mixtures and to identify the components with greater accuracy.

◀ Forensic scientists use chromatography to identify the different substances present at the scene of a crime.

TEST YOURSELF

▶ A team of forensic scientists wish to match the paint pigment found at the scene of a crime with the pigment from the cars of three suspects. The chromatograms are shown below.

Which suspect would the forensic scientists tell the police about and which could they eliminate? Explain your answers.

(1) Sample from the crime scene

(2) Suspect A

(3) Suspect B

(4) Suspect C

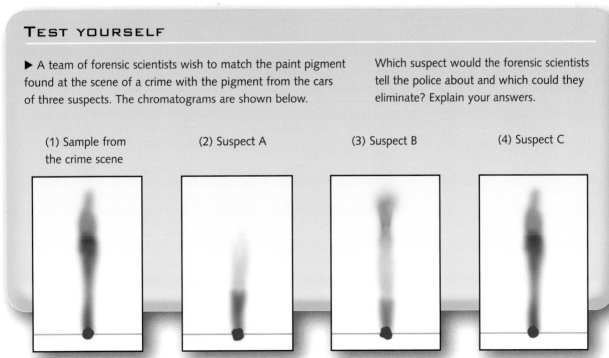

Glossary

ALCHEMY – The ancient study of chemistry.

ALPHA PARTICLES – Particles that contain two neutrons and two protons.

ATOM – The simplest form of a particle.

ATOMIC NUMBER – The number of protons in an atom of an element.

BCE – Before Common Era. The Common Era (CE), is the period of measured time beginning with the year 1 (the traditional birthdate of Jesus).

BOILING – Changing from a liquid to a gas.

BONDING – Joining together of two or more atoms through a chemical reaction.

BROWNIAN MOTION – The random movement of particles in air or a fluid, first observed through a microscope by Robert Brown in 1827.

CHROMATOGRAPHY – A method of separating mixtures, using a solvent.

COMPOUND – A substance made from at least two different elements chemically bonded together.

CONDENSATION – Changing from a gas to a liquid. Condensation occurs when gases are cooled.

CONTRACT – When a material becomes smaller.

DENSITY – A measure of mass with volume.

DISTILLATION – Separating a substance through boiling and cooling.

ELECTRON – The negative part of an atom. Electrons travel in shells.

ELECTRON CONFIGURATION – The arrangement of electrons in an atom.

EVAPORATION – Changing from a liquid to a gas.

EXPAND – When a material becomes larger.

FRACTIONAL DISTILLATION – Separating several substances using boiling.

ANSWERS

p12 Investigate
(1) Magnesium – atomic number 12, mass number 24 (12 protons, 12 electrons, 12 neutrons)

(2) Bromine – atomic number 35, mass number 80 (35 protons, 35 electrons, 45 neutrons)

(3) Neon – atomic number 10, mass number 20 (10 protons, 10 electrons, 10 neutrons)

p15 Test yourself
Aluminium has 13 protons (and therefore 13 electrons). The first shell has 2 electrons (the maximum) leaving 11 remaining. The second shell has 8 electrons (the maximum) leaving 3 remaining. The third shell contains the remaining 3 electrons and is not completely full. The electron configuration for aluminium is therefore 2.8.3.

p15 Investigate
(1) Neon – atomic number 10, electron configuration 2.8.
(2) Magnesium – atomic number 12, electron configuration 2.8.2.
(3) Calcium – atomic number 20, electron configuration 2.8.10.
(4) Chlorine – atomic number 17, electron configuration 2.8.7.
(5) Sodium – atomic number 11, electron configuration 2.8.1.

p17 Test yourself
(1) Jelly – wobbles and not very strong; can be poured when heated.
(2) Adhesive paste - spread on the back of wallpaper but when set becomes hard like a solid.
(3) Glue stick – in the tube it is solid, but when rubbed across paper, a sticky residue is left behind.

p23 Investigate
(1) Na – Sodium   (5) Scandium – Sc
(2) Mg – Magnesium   (6) Sulphur – S
(3) Zn – Zinc   (7) Antimony – Sb
(4) I – Iodine   (8) Lead – Pb

p25 Investigate
You should find that your predictions are generally correct, but that the properties are either more exaggerated for groups on the left or less exaggerated for groups on the right (as you go down the group).

p27 Investigate
Argon (Ar) and potassium (K); cobalt (Co) and nickel (Ni); thorium (Th) and protactinium (Pa).

p33 Investigate
You should find that the mass is approximately the

FREE RADICALS – Particles that contain electrons that are unpaired.

FREEZING – Changing from a liquid to a solid.

FUSION – The joining together of nuclei.

GROUP – A vertical collection of elements in the Periodic Table.

INTERMOLECULAR – Between molecules.

IONS – Particles with either a positive or negative charge.

MASS NUMBER – The number of protons and neutrons that an atom contains.

MELTING – Changing from a solid to a liquid.

MOLECULE – At least two atoms chemically bonded together.

NEUTRINO – An elementary particle.

NEUTRON – The part of a nucleus that contains no charge.

NUCLEUS – The central part of an atom containing neutrons and protons.

PERIOD – A horizontal collection of elements in the Periodic Table.

PERIODIC TABLE – A table showing all of the chemical elements.

PROTON – The positive part of an atom, found in the nucleus.

RADIOACTIVE – The breakdown of atoms through natural processes.

SUBLIMATION – Changing directly from a solid to a gas (or the other way around).

VOLATILE – Easily evaporated.

Useful websites:

www.bbc.co.uk/schools
www.chem4kids.com
www.sciencenewsforkids.org
www.newscientist.com
www.howstuffworks.com

same, but the volume is much greater in ice than in water.

p33 Test yourself
(1) Condensation
(2) Evaporation

p34 Test yourself
As you blow into the balloon the number of air particles inside is increased and the pressure increases. Eventually the pressure is too great to contain the air particles and the balloon bursts.

The same number of particles occupy a larger space so the number of collisions with the walls of the container are reduced. This reduces the pressure.

p36 Test yourself
(1) Shaving foam – gas/liquid.
(2) White coffee with no sugar – liquid/liquid.

(3) White coffee with sugar – liquid/liquid and liquid/solid.
(4) Coin – solid/solid.

p38 Test yourself
(1) Sodium and hydroxide (NaOH – sodium hydroxide).
(2) Magnesium and chloride ($MgCl_2$ – magnesium chloride).
(3) Calcium and oxide (CaO – calcium oxide).

p39 Investigate
(1) Fleming left a Petri dish on a window sill and mould grew in his absence.
(2) Antibiotics have saved lives all over the world, but resistance is becoming commonplace because many antibiotics have been over-used. Bacteria that become resistant to antibiotics given to animals, for example, can pass to humans via the food chain.

(3) Chemists can use the structure of the original penicillin and synthesise similar compounds. These drugs are just as effective, and bacteria are not resistant to them.

p42 Investigate
You will probably observe white crystals that taste salty.

p45 Investigate
Darker colours, such as brown, will contain more colours than the lighter colours, such as yellow.

p45 Test yourself
Suspect C should be arrested because the chromatogram is exactly the same as the sample from the crime scene. Suspect A is eliminated because there is a light blue colour present (and no red/pink). Suspect B is eliminated because there is a light blue colour present.

Index